Advent Calendar for Adults

24 Days of Brain-Tickling Riddles & Fun Activities to Solve Before Christmas

IQ Street

ISBN: 979-8-89095-061-1

Introduction

'Tis the season to be jolly, as the old Christmas carol goes. And if there's one thing guaranteed to make your holiday period just a little bit jollier, then it's some festive-themed fun and games!

Welcome to your Advent Calendar! Over the next 24 days, as we count down toward Christmas Day, this book will bring you a mix of festive trivia and strange-but-true stories, alongside some suitably Christmassy brainteasers and word games designed to give your gray matter a little workout too. Simply check back into this book every day between December 1 and Christmas Eve to tackle your next round of facts, trivia, and festive fun.

The book is arranged in order, day by day, just like a regular advent calendar. Each day will begin with a festive joke or brainteasing riddle, followed by a quick puzzle or trivia quiz. Simply turn the page for the solutions to these quizzes and games—and for one last bit of festive fun, either in the form of some fast did-you-know facts, or an interesting strange-but-true story.

Like all good advent calendars, though, don't get impatient and flick ahead a day or two! The book is designed to be enjoyed one day at a time—so don't be tempted to peek ahead at what's to come! After all, Christmas Day will be here before you know it...

December 1

When Dasher was eight, Rudolph was half his age. Now, Dasher is 14. How old is Rudolph?

Word Game

CHRISTMAS MAD LIB

Follow the directions to come up with a Santa's List like no other...

Dear Santa,

The year is coming to an end, and I am feeling very

[ADJECTIVE] *. This year, I have been a really,*

[ADJECTIVE] [NOUN] *doing lots of extra*

jobs to help around the [PLACE] *. I even*

helped my , [RELATIVE OR PERSON YOU KNOW] *,* [NAME] *to*

[VERB] *their* [NOUN] *!*

So, I think I deserve my favorite first choice

present—a brand new [NOUN] *. If there is*

room on your [NOUN] *, I'd also love for you to*

bring me a [COLOR] [NOUN] *!*

If you did, I'd feel so [ADJECTIVE] *on*

Christmas morning!

Did you know?

- Santa's reindeer were first named in a poem published in 1823.
- Queen Elizabeth I once celebrated Christmas by having miniature gingerbread effigies made of members of her court.
- The name Rudolph literally means "famous wolf"!
- The first commercial Christmas cards emerged in the Victorian era...
- ...but they were a lot different from the cards we send today and often featured cartoonish depictions of morality tales. Popular images included dead birds, a child with a flaming pudding for a head, and marching armies of armed frogs!
- The "nog" in eggnog is an old English word for strong ale or liquor.

Solutions

Riddle: 10.

If six years ago Rudolph was half of eight (four), he must be 10 now.

December 2

What might you find under the sea, in the sky, and on a Christmas tree?

Word Game

FINISH THE PHRASE

Do you recognize these festive phrases and sayings? See if you can finish each line off correctly!

1. *Peace on Earth, and good will to all ...*

2. *On the eighth day of Christmas, my true love gave to me eight ...*

3. *Bells on bobtails ring, making ...*

4. *I will honor Christmas in my heart, and try to keep it ...*

5. *Then the Grinch thought of something he hadn't before! What if Christmas, he thought, doesn't come from ...*

6. *Away in a manger, no crib for a bed, the little Lord Jesus ...*

Did you know?

- Rudolph was added to the traditional list of Santa's reindeer in 1939, as part of a marketing ploy by US retailer Montgomery Ward.
- Around half of all Americans will attend church on either Christmas Day or Christmas Eve.
- One of the earliest known gingerbread recipes, dating back to the 1400s, didn't contain any ginger...
- ...instead, the warming flavor of the bread was replicated using a mixture of boiled honey, saffron, and pepper.
- According to the *Guinness Book of Records*, the world's oldest artificial Christmas tree is owned by a British man named Paul Parker, whose family have used the same tree every year since 1886!
- A single snowflake is typically comprised of roughly 200 individual ice crystals.

Solutions

RIDDLE: A star

FINISH THE PHRASE

1. ...men. (*Luke, 2:14*)
2. ...maids a-milking. ("The Twelve Days of Christmas")
3. ...spirits bright. ("Jingle Bells")
4. ...all the year. (Charles Dickens, *A Christmas Carol*)
5. ...a store. (Dr. Seuss, *How the Grinch Stole Christmas*)
6. ...laid down His sweet head. (*"Away in a Manger"*)

December 3

What's the hardest thing about learning how to ice skate?

Word Game

CHRISTMAS TRIVIA

Let's test your knowledge of all things festive with this quick Christmas trivia quiz!

Q. ***Which of Santa's reindeer has a name that means a flash of light in German?***

A. Donner
B. Vixen
C. Dasher
D. Blitzen

Q. ***In what modern-day country is St. Nicholas believed to have been born?***

A. China
B. Egypt
C. Turkey
D. Sweden

Q. ***Which famous poet wrote the lyrics to the Christmas carol "In the Bleak Midwinter"?***

A. Robert Frost
B. Christina Rossetti
C. Robert Burns
D. Emily Brontë

Did you know?

* Christmas is celebrated by two billion people around the world each year.
* The song "White Christmas" stayed at Number one on the Billboard charts for 11 weeks in 1942...
* ...and returned to the top of the charts in Christmas 1943 and 1944 too!
* The poem *A Visit From St. Nicholas* was written by Clement Clarke Moore—who was a professor of Greek literature at a New York school!
* Mistletoe is poisonous.
* Christmas is abbreviated to Xmas because the Greek letter chi—the first letter of "Christ" in Greek—is shaped like an X.
* The first commercial Christmas cards were sold in the 1840s.

Solutions

RIDDLE: The ice!

CHRISTMAS TRIVIA

D. Blitzen

C. Turkey

B. Christina Rossetti

December 4

What does a snowman become when it's old?

Word Game

TWO TRUTHS AND A LIE

In each of the rounds below, two of the statements are correct, but there is one imposter. Can you guess the lie hiding among the truths?

1. ST. NICHOLAS

A. St. Nicholas is a patron saint of children

B. St. Nicholas is a patron saint of brewers

C. St. Nicholas is a patron saint of embroiderers

2. CHRISTMAS TURKEYS

A. A male turkey is called a "gobbler"

B. A female turkey is called a "nanny"

C. A flock of turkeys is called a "rafter"

3. "O HOLY NIGHT"

A. "O Holy Night" was written in America

B. "O Holy Night" is over 150 years old

C. "O Holy Night" was originally a poem

Did you know?

THE ETYMOLOGY OF MISTLETOE

It's one of the world's most popular and familiar Christmas decorations, but did you know that the origin of the name "mistletoe"—well, leaves a lot to be desired?

In fact, the name mistletoe derives from two Old English roots, *missel* (which is the plant's original name) and *tan* (meaning a small branch or twig). Where that name *missel* comes from, though, is something of a mystery. But according to some language historians, it is related to an even older word for dung, or animal waste. Put those two roots together, ultimately, and the ever-romantic Christmas staple of mistletoe has a name essentially literally meaning "poop twig!"

To understand quite why the plant earned that name, we need to know a little bit more about its nature. Oddly, mistletoe is a parasitic plant, meaning that it doesn't have roots in the ground but rather takes its nutriment from other host plants and trees, into which it burrows its modified root stalks instead. It's for that reason that bunches of mistletoe are often found high up in the tops of trees, rather than growing on the ground.

How does the plant get up there, though? Well, the plant's seeds are propagated in its characteristic white berries, which are greedily consumed by hungry fruit-eating birds. The birds then digest the fruit but pass out the hard seed at its center—often while perched at the top of a tree. So long as it lands in a favorable patch, close to the tree's bark and with enough sunshine to nourish it, the mistletoe can then grow once more to begin the extraordinary (if a little unusual!) cycle all over again.

Solutions

RIDDLE: A pool of water!

TWO TRUTHS AND A LIE

C. Embroiderers.
St. Nicholas is also a patron saint of barrel-makers, fishermen, merchants, and pharmacists.

B. A nanny.
A female turkey is actually known as a "hen."

A. O Holy Night was written in America.
It was actually written in France.

December 5

Describe Santa's sack on December 26 using just two letters.

Word Game

FINISH THE PHRASE

Do you recognize these festive phrases and sayings? See if you can finish each line off correctly!

1. *Over the hills we go, ...*

2. *All is calm, all is ...*

3. *It is the night of the dear Savior's ...*

4. *It came without ribbons, it came without ...*

5. *Later, we'll have some pumpkin pie, and we'll ...*

6. *Christmas time is coming soon! Now, you dear old man, whisper ...*

Did you know?

- London's famous Victorian and Albert Museum houses a collection of 300,000 historical Christmas cards.
- Reindeers' hooves become harder in winter to help them walk over frozen ground.
- The average snowflake falls from the sky at around 3mph.
- The record for the number of Christmas baubles suspended in a man's beard is 710!
- Shakespeare's *Twelfth Night* is his most festive play, but Christmas isn't mentioned in it once...
- ...In fact, Shakespeare only mentioned Christmas three times in his plays: once in *The Taming of the Shrew*, and twice in *Love's Labour's Lost*.

Solutions

RIDDLE: M–T!

FINISH THE PHRASE

1. ...laughing all the way. ("Jingle Bells")
2. ...bright. ("Silent NIght")
3. ...birth ("O Holy Night")
4. ...tags (Dr. Seus, *How the Grinch Stole Christmas*)
5. ...do some caroling. (Brenda Lee, "Rockin' Around the Christmas Tree")
6. ...what you'll bring to me. ("Jolly Old St. NIcholas")

December 6

What makes Christmas trees so bad at sewing?

Word Game

CRYPTOGRAM

In this Christmas Cryptogram, every letter in a suitably festive joke has been replaced by another. Working letter by letter, can you return the joke to its original form?

U E F Y G X F O W F D J O

_ _ A _ _ S _ _ E _ _ _ F

X F S Y F V N F P X V F N N W B

_ _ N _ _ _ _ _ U _ _ _ L _ _ ?

V N F P X Y D J I E J H G F !

_ _ _ _ _ _ _ _ _ H _ _ _ _ !

Did you know?

* Reindeer antlers can have more than 40 individual points.

* The world's largest Christmas stocking was made in Italy in 2011. It was over 168 ft long!

* Jim Carrey's *How the Grinch Stole Christmas* is the highest-grossing Christmas movie of all time.

* The average American will spend $900 each Christmas.

* Croatians drink a type of infused mistletoe brandy called "biska."

* The first Christmas candy canes were made in Germany.

Solutions

RIDDLE: They're always dropping their needles!

CRYPTOGRAM: What is a fear of Santa Claus called? Claustrophobia!

December 7

Where does Christmas come before Thanksgiving, summer, and Easter?

Word Game

ANAGRAMS

Can you unjumble these festive anagrams?

1. SLANCED

2. PUR HOLD

3. RAMSSCUL

4. I GLESH

5. GIN COLAR

6. COORDINATES

Did you know?

* In her teens, the future Queen Victoria is known to have served her favorite pet spaniel two pieces of gingerbread, surrounded by holly leaves, as a Christmas present.
* "Thundersnow" is a rare atmospheric condition in which it snows during a thunderstorm!
* A reindeer can migrate as much as 3,000 miles each year in search of food during the winter.
* The world's largest Christmas bauble was put on display in Dubai in 2018. It had a diameter of over 15ft!
* Around two-fifths of people start their Christmas shopping in October.
* More than half of items ordered online during the holiday period are ordered on an app.

Solutions

RIDDLE: In the dictionary

ANAGRAMS

1. Candles
2. Rudolph
3. Mrs. Claus
4. Sleigh
5. Caroling
6. Decorations

December 8

What does a reindeer have that a caribou doesn't—and December have that none of the other months do?

Word Game

FINISH THE PHRASE

Do you recognize these festive phrases and sayings? See if you can finish each line off correctly!

1. *Holy infant so ...*

2. *Fall on your knees! O, hear the angel ...*

3. *Dashing through the snow, in a ...*

4. *The Grinch hated Christmas — the whole Christmas season. Oh, please don't ask why, no one quite knows...*

5. *You will get a sentimental feelin' when you hear voices singing ...*

6. *Good King Wenceslas looked out on the ...*

Did you know?

WHY WE HANG STOCKINGS

Hanging stockings by the chimney—which we wake on Christmas morning to find stuffed with treats and presents—is not only one of the most quintessential of holiday decorations, it's also one of many people's fondest childhood memories of Christmases gone by. But why do we do it?

This is one of the peculiar mysteries of Christmas lore that historians have argued over for decades. Although we might not have a definitive explanation of our Christmas stocking-hanging tradition, we do, however, have a fairly reliable theory, that stems from one the central figures in the holiday period, St. Nicholas.

No spoilers—we'll come to the real St. Nicholas a little later in our Christmas countdown—but for now all we need to know is that he was a charitable and benevolent figure in early church of medieval Europe, who dedicated his life to sharing the wealth of his church with the poorest people in his congregation. Various tales and legends abound of St. Nicholas' generosity, but one story of his benevolence that people come back to time and again is that of three poor daughters of a local widower.

According to the tale, the daughters had done their washing one day, and had retired to bed that evening while their stockings and other garments dried by the smoldering fire. Nicholas, wanting to help the bereaved family out with an anonymous gift, sneaked up onto the roof of the house and dropped three parcels of gold down the chimney, which promptly (and unbeknownst to him) landed in the girls' stockings.

The following morning, the three sisters awoke to find the gifts waiting for them, establishing a tradition that we still observe today.

Solutions

RIDDLE: A letter D

FINISH THE PHRASE

1. ...tender and mild. ("Silent Night")
2. ...voices. ("O Holy NIght")
3. ...one horse open sleigh. ("Jingle Bells")
4. ...the reason. (Dr. Seuss, *How the Grinch Stole Christmas*)
5. ... "Let's be jolly! Deck the halls with boughs of holly!" (Brenda Lee, "Rockin' Around the Christmas Tree")
6. ...feast of Stephen. ("Good King Wenceslas")

December 9

What kind of festive bird has a shell?

Word Game

CHRISTMAS MAD LIB

Follow the directions below to come up with a Christmas cake recipe like nothing you've ever made before!

First of all, you need a sufficiently large bowl—about large enough to put a ______ (NOUN) *in should be fine.*

Then, assemble your ingredients: flour, sugar, eggs, butter, dried fruit, ______ (NOUN)*, and of course, lots and lots of* ______ (ADJECTIVE) ______ (NOUN)*!*

Sift the flour into a ______ (CONTAINER)*, then mix in the sugar, butter, fruit, and eggs using a* ______ (NOUN)*.*

You might want to throw in a dash of ______ (FOOD) *too for extra flavor.*

Once everything is mixed together, transfer the mix into a

ADJECTIVE	CONTAINER

, and then bake in the

oven for

NUMBER	LENGTH OF TIME

.

Once cooked, wrap the cake in parchment paper and store it

in [PLACE] *for* [NUMBER] *days.*

Serve at Christmastime with lots of [FOOD] *!*

Did you know?

- Some herds of reindeer can have as many as half a million animals in them.
- 96% of people buy Christmas presents for their families.
- The ancient Druids of Europe thought mistletoe was an aphrodisiac, and used it as a medicine.
- Julesild—a kind of spiced pickled herring—is a traditional festive meal in Denmark.
- Tinsel was originally made from real silver.
- When approached to play Scrooge in the *Muppets Christmas Carol*, Michael Caine told the director that he would only accept the role if he could play it completely straight, as if the Muppets were the Royal Shakespeare Company!

Solutions

RIDDLE: A turtle dove

December 10

What would you find in outer space and in front of Santa's sleigh?

Word Game

TWO TRUTHS AND A LIE

In each of the rounds below, two of the statements are correct, but there is one imposter. Can you guess the lie hiding among the truths?

1. CANDY CANES

A. Candy canes haven't always been J shaped

B. Candy canes were invented in China

C. Candy canes only got their characteristic red stripe around 100 years ago

2. "JINGLE BELLS"

A. "Jingle Bells" was originally written to be sung on Thanksgiving

B. "Jingle Bells" only has two verses

C. "Jingle Bells" was the first song played in space

3. REINDEER

A. Reindeer live in both the Arctic and Antarctic

B. Both male and female reindeer have antlers

C. Reindeer don't eat meat

Did you know?

* In Canada, Santa has his own postcode for his letters every year. It's H0H 0H0.

* On average, men spend around 10% more money on Christmas presents than women.

* According to a 2024 survey, the most popular ingredient in a Christmas dinner is roast potatoes.

* Reindeer have two layers of fur, which works to trap warm air against their bodies to keep them warm...

* ...This adaptation also makes them especially buoyant, allowing them to cross rivers and open water with relative ease!

* The US postal service handles around 12 billion items of mail during the holiday season alone.

Solutions

RIDDLE: Comet!

TWO TRUTHS AND A LIE

1. B. Candy canes were invented in China.
   The first candy canes were actually made in Germany.
2. B. "Jingle Bells" only has two verses.
   Actually, it has several, with different versions of the song having four or more.
3. A. Reindeer live in both the Arctic and Antarctic.
   Reindeer only live in the far north of the northern hemisphere, across North America, Europe, and Asia.

December 11

Why can't you take back the things you cover in gift wrap?

Word Game

ANAGRAMS

Can you unjumble these festive anagrams?

1. BASBLEU

2. ITVANITY

3. SERPENTS

4. GLEANS

5. A DANCY NEC

6. STUN TECHS

Did you know?

- The most common Christmas present in America is a gift card.
- The retractable dance floor above a swimming pool used in the festive movie *It's A Wonderful Life* still exists, and is still in use at Beverly Hills High School in California.
- The centerpiece of Christmas dinner in Brazil is often a dish of salted cod.
- "Feuerzangenbowle" is a kind of German mulled wine, flavored with drops of boozy molten sugar. Its name literally means "fire-tongs punch."
- Bing Crosby's "White Christmas" has sold over 100 million copies worldwide.
- Reindeer's eyes change color in the winter, allowing them to see better in the lower light of the Arctic night.

Solutions

RIDDLE: Because they're in the present!

ANAGRAMS

1. Baubles
2. Nativity
3. Presents
4. Angels
5. Candy cane
6. Chestnuts

December 12

What will you find at the top of a stocking, and the very end of Christmas?

Word Game

CHRISTMAS TRIVIA QUIZ

Let's test your knowledge of all things festive with this quick Christmas trivia quiz!

Q. *In the famous story A Visit from St. Nicholas, "not a creature was stirring—not even a ..." what?*

A. Cat
B. Dog
C. Mouse
D. Spider

Q. *What festive item might be placed in a chamberstick?*

A. Candy cane
B. Spring of mistletoe
C. Bell
D. Candle

Q. *"Inkberry" and "possumhaw" are the names of different types of what festive plant?*

A. Holly
B. Ivy
C. Mistletoe
D. Pine

Did you know?

THE FIRST CHRISTMAS TREES

It's hard to imagine Christmastime without Christmas trees, but incredibly our version of this tradition is barely 200 years old.

True, people have been decorating the inside of their houses with evergreen branches and foliage for thousands of years, with even the Ancient Egyptians believed to have used palm fronds and similar greenery to decorate their homes during the wintertime as a symbol of the eventual return of spring. The Romans did much the same with wreaths of laurel and olive, which were also used as symbols of victory, peace, and happiness in the ancient world.

That tradition was turned on its head in medieval Europe when, rather than bringing green boughs indoors as decorations, the trees themselves were adorned. In 15th-century Germany, for instance, bakers in the city of Freiberg are known to have decorated trees with sweet pastries and Christmas gingerbreads. And in what is now Riga, the capital city of Latvia in northeast Europe, a band of local merchants in the 16th century used roses—symbols of the Virgin Mary—to decorate a tree in the city center, before promptly setting it alight and dancing around it as a kind of festive bonfire. Thankfully, we're not quite so keen to set fire to our Christmas trees today, of course!

Our more modern traditional Christmas tree likewise emerged in central Europe, with festive revelers in Germany continuing the bakers' tradition of decorating a tree with Christmas treats. By the 19th century, it had become commonplace to add candles, baubles, and other glittering trinkets and ornaments to the tree too—and when Britain's Queen Victoria married a German prince, Albert of Saxe-Coburg and Gotha, in 1840, he brought this tradition to England with him.

Although Queen Victoria's German grandmother, Princess Charlotte, the wife of George III, had also brought decorated trees to England some decades earlier, the tradition did not catch on until the mid 1800s. That's partly because of the reach of the press by that time, which could circulate information far more rapidly than ever before, and also due to the young queen's popularity among the British people. By modern standards, it's hard to appreciate just how popular Queen Victoria was in 19th-century England, but it's safe to say that whatever she and her household did soon became the talk of London, and the latest fashion across Britain as a whole. So when drawings of the royal family decorating a tree with candles and other adornments landed in the papers of Victorian England, the traditional Christmas tree caught on like wildfire. It has remained the cornerstone of our festive decorations ever since.

Solutions

RIDDLE: The letter S

CHRISTMAS TRIVIA QUIZ

1. C. Mouse
2. D. Candle

   A chamberstick is a small candle holder, set in a flat dish held by a loop around a finger.
3. A. Holly

   Inkberry is another name for the plant also called Canadian winterberry or Appalachian tea, while possumhaw is meadow holly.

December 13

Where does Frosty the Snowman keep his money?

Word Game

FINISH THE PHRASE

Do you recognize these festive phrases and sayings? See if you can finish each line off correctly!

1. *Glories stream from heaven afar, Heavenly hosts sing ...*

2. *He puzzled and puzzled till his puzzler ...*

3. *Everyone dancin' merrily in the new ...*

4. *I'm dreaming of a white Christmas with every ...*

5. *And if you ever saw it, you would even say it ...*

6. *Chestnuts roasting on an open fire, Jack Frost ...*

Did you know?

* When writer Robert May needed a name of Santa's red-nosed leading reindeer in 1939, he initially toyed with Rollo, Romeo, and Reginald before landing on Rudolph!
* The circular shape of a Christmas wreath is a religious symbol, intended to represent the continued life of God and Jesus at Christmastime.
* Christmas was not made a federal holiday in the United States until 1870 under President Grant.
* The average homemade serving of eggnog has an alcohol content of just under 9% ABV.
* Every year in the US, over 18,00 people end up in the emergency room having had an accident decorating hanging Christmas decorations...
* ...with the most common accident a fall from a ladder—records of which are six times higher than normal during the holiday period!

Solutions

RIDDLE: In a snowbank

FINISH THE PHRASE

1. ...allelulia. ("Silent Night")
2. ...was sore. (Dr. Seuss, *How the Grinch Stole Christmas*)
3. ...old-fashioned way. (Brenda Lee, "Rockin' Around the Christmas Tree")
4. ...Christmas card I write. (Bing Crosby, "White Christmas")
5. ...glows. ("Rudolph the Red-Nosed Reindeer")
6. ...nipping at your nose. (Nat King Cole, "The Christmas Song")

December 14

I'm a ball you might see at Christmas, but I cannot be bounced—and I probably shouldn't be held indoors! What am I?

Word Game

CRYPTOGRAM

In this Christmas Cryptogram, every letter in a suitably festive joke has been replaced by another. Working letter by letter, can you return the joke to its original form?

X N Z Z   J Y   W Y L   E Z F F   Z M

_ H _ _   _ O   _ _ _   _ _ L _   A _

Y Q M Y P G Y L T   H I G M J I I H ?

_ _ N _ _ _ _ _ S   _ _ I _ _ _ E _ ?

H L J I - J Y F S N !

R _ _ _ - D _ _ _ _ !

Did you know?

- "Jingle Bells" was originally titled "One Horse Open Sleigh."
- During Puritan times, celebrating Christmas was illegal and was even punishable by a fine in the mid 1600s.
- On average, Canadian spend more on Christmas than Americans.
- Nativity scenes in Catalonia, in northern Spain, typically feature a character called "the Canager"—which is almost always depicted going to the toilet in the corner of the stable!
- The word "troll" in the line "Troll the ancient Yuletide carol" is an old word meaning "to sing loudly."
- In 2024, "O Holy Night" was voted the UK's most popular Christmas carol for a record ninth year in a row.

Solutions

RIDDLE: A snowball

CRYPTOGRAM

What do you call an obnoxious reindeer? Rude-dolph!

December 15

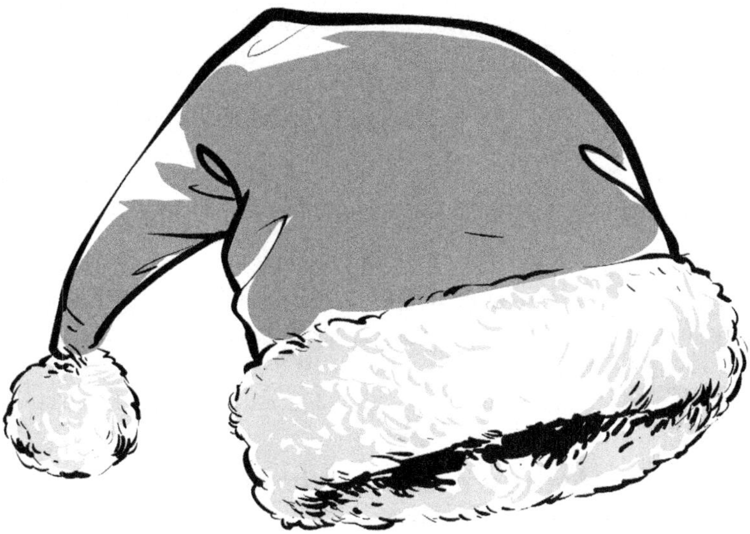

I'm a toe that you'll not find in a stocking, nor on someone's feet. You will see me at Christmastime, though. What am I?

Word Game

CHRISTMAS MAD LIB

How to put up the perfect Christmas tree—mad lib style!

Seeing a beautifully decorated Christmas tree always makes me feel [FEELING] *. So, here's my perfect method for decorating a tree that would make anybody say* [EXCLAMATION] *! First of all, you need the perfect sized tree: one about* [NUMBER] [MEASUREMENT] *tall should be fine. Make sure it has plenty of* [NOUNS] *too. Chop the tree down using a* [NOUN] *, then stand it upright in your* [ROOM] *. Start with the lights on the tree first—you'll want to wrap those around, forming big* [SHAPES] *as you go. Then hang the tinsel, then the baubles—I like baubles that are*

COLOR ______ *and* SHAPE ______ *the best!*

Lastly, put a NOUN ______ *on top of the tree to complete the look. You'll be feeling* FEELING ______ *when you see it on Christmas morning surrounded by* NOUNS ______ *!*

Did you know?

- The word "tinsel" comes from a French word meaning to sparkle.
- Around three-quarters of all the money a person spends on Christmas is spent on presents.
- In Belgium in 2010, a single Christmas tree was decorated with over 194,000 individual lights!
- It might be set during wintertime, but *It's A Wonderful Life* was filmed during a California heatwave in the summer of 1946...
- ...in fact, it got so hot on set one day, that director Franz Capra had to shoot the set down and send everyone home early to recover!
- The word "Christmas" is a literal one: etymologically, it literally means "the mass on Christ's day."

Solutions

RIDDLE: Mistletoe

December 16

Santa had to pay five cents to park his sleigh. Who is he now?

Word Game

TWO TRUTHS AND A LIE

In each of the rounds below, two of the statements are correct, but there is one imposter. Can you guess the lie hiding among the truths?

1. *GINGERBREAD MEN*

A. Gingerbread was once used to treat upset stomachs

B. Germany was once the gingerbread capital of the world

C. Henry VIII hated gingerbread

2. *SNOWMEN*

A. Building a snowman burns around 200 calories an hour

B. The world's tallest snowman was 22 ft tall

C. According to experts, the best snowmen need at least four inches of snowfall

3. *CHRISTMAS TREES*

A. Nearly 99% of all the world's Christmas trees come from tree farms

B. The Christmas tree displayed in Trafalgar Square, London, each year is a gift from Norway

C. It can take more than five years for a Christmas tree to grow to 6ft tall

Did you know?

THE HISTORY OF JINGLE BELLS

One of the most popular Christmas songs, "Jingle Bells" was written by an American songwriter and musician named James Lord Pierpont in 1857.

Born in Boston in 1822, Pierpont was a pastor, a staunch abolitionist, and an amateur poet. In the 1840s, he left Massachusetts for California and spent a brief time in San Francisco during the Gold Rush. On his return east, he began using his poetic skills to compose songs reminiscing and romanticizing his time out west, publishing a collection of his work in 1852.

Over the years that followed, Pierpont continued to write songs, hymns, ballads, and even minstrel songs, before finally writing the tune we now know as "Jingle Bells" in Boston in 1857. Having no idea how much of a holiday staple his song would become, by the time the song was published and copyrighted, Pierpont had moved to join his brother at a church in Georgia, where we became the local organist. He remained in the South for the rest of his life, before his death in Florida in 1893—just a few years after some of the earliest known recordings of "Jingle Bells" began to appear.

One of the very first versions of Jingle Bells we know of was recorded by a banjoist named Will Lyle in 1889. The earliest surviving recording, made by a vocal group called the Edison Male Quartette, dates from 1898. But it wasn't until 1902, when the famous Hayden Quartet of singers covered the song, that its popularity quickly took off.

By the 1910s, "Jingle Bells" had already become a popular holiday standard, and as more and more artists covered it—including Benny Goodman in 1935, and Glenn Miller in 1941—its popularity continued to rise. By 1965, the song had even become well known enough to become the first song ever broadcast from outer space, when Gemini 6 astronauts Tom Stafford and Wally Schirra performed an impromptu version (they smuggled a harmonica on board their craft) for mission control, having reported sighting "an object ... in polar orbit" from their window!

Solutions

RIDDLE: St. Nickel-less

TWO TRUTHS AND A LIE

1. C. Henry VIII hated gingerbread.
   In fact, gingerbread was a staple at Tudor-period feasts, and Henry is known to have appreciated its warming herbal and medicinal properties.
2. B. The world's tallest snowman was 22 ft tall.
   Actually, it was 122 ft tall!
3. It can take more than five years for a Christmas tree to grow to 6ft tall. It actually takes around 10 years.

December 17

Which of Santa's reindeer knows Morse Code?

Word Game

FINISH THE PHRASE

Do you recognize these festive phrases and sayings?
See if you can finish each line off correctly!

1. *A thrill of hope, the weary world ...*

2. *Mistletoe hung where you can ...*

3. *On the ninth day of Christmas, my true love gave to me nine ...*

4. *Hark! the herald angels sing, "Glory to the ..."*

5. *Where the treetops glisten and children ...*

6. *Everybody knows a turkey and some mistletoe help to ...*

Did you know?

- Using evergreen boughs as wintertime decorations is a practice thought to date back via the Romans to Ancient Egypt. The Egyptians would use green palm fronds as seasonal decorations as a symbol of the eventual return of spring.
- There are three times as many domestic and captive bred reindeer in Europe than there are in the wild.
- As well as evergreen branches, a traditional Christmas wreath should also be decorated with 24 candles—one for each day of the festive period.
- In Germany, it's traditional to hang a glass pickle on the Christmas tree.
- Christmas island, in Australia, is so named because it was discovered on Christmas Day in 1643.
- Contrary to popular belief, Santa's red coat and trousers weren't the work of the Coca-Cola company. They may have popularized the look, but Santa had been depicted wearing red—along with many other colors—for centuries by the time Coca-Cola started using him in their adverts in the early 1900s!

Solutions

RIDDLE: Dasher

FINISH THE PHRASE

1. ...rejoices. ("O Holy Night")
2. ...see. (Brenda Lee, "Rockin' Aroumd the Christmas Tree")
3. ...ladies dancing. ("The Twelve Days of Christmas")
4. ..."newborn king." ("Hark! The Herald Angels Sing")
5. ...listen. (Bing Crosby, 'White Christmas")
6. ...make the seasons bright. (Nat King Cole, "The Christmas Song")

December 18

Why is Christmastime the best time to improve your AC?

Word Game

CHRISTMAS TRIVIA QUIZ

Let's test your knowledge of all things festive with this quick Christmas trivia quiz!

Q. ***On what date of the festive period is it traditional to open presents in some Spanish and Latin American countries?***

A. December 24 **B.** December 26

C. January 31 **D.** January 6

Q. ***Which of these is another name for a reindeer?***

A. Marabou **B.** Caribou

C. Kinkajou **D.** Tinamou

Q. ***How many "swans a-swimming" are there in the traditional "Twelve Days of Christmas"?***

A. Four **B.** Six

C. Seven **D.** Eleven

Did you know?

- Reindeer have a higher-than-normal concentration of fatty acid in their feet to stop them from freezing in the snow!
- The world's tallest Christmas tree was 212 ft tall.
- A traditional Catalan Spanish Christmas lunch begins with a meal of a pasta-filled meat soup called "sopa de galets."
- The six central prongs of a snowflake are properly called "branches."
- The popular "Christmas Song", recorded by Nat King Cole, was written by legendary songwriter Mel Tormé in a blisteringly hot summer in 1945. He later said he wrote the song in an effort "to stay cool by thinking cool."
- In Japan, it is traditional to eat a KFC dinner on Christmas Day.

Solutions

RIDDLE: Because it's ad-vent!

CHRISTMAS TRIVIA QUIZ

1. D. January 6

   Although many people still celebrate Christmas, the highlight of the festive period is Epiphany, at the start of January.

2. B. Caribou

   A marabou is a kind of stork, a kinkajou is a kind of coati-like mammal of the rainforest, and a tinamou is a kind of Latin American grouse-like bird.

3. C. Seven

   There are four calling birds, six geese a laying, and 11 pipers piping.

December 19

What does Santa have instead of a walking stick?

Word Game

ANAGRAMS

Can you unjumble these festive anagrams?

1. TEVAND

2. SLIMETOTE

3. YINCHEM

4. MONAWNS

5. THAWER

6. LAND RACE

Did you know?

* Unlike other species of deer, reindeer have fur even on the tips of their noses—so even Rudolph's nose would have been covered in hair! The adaptation helps them keep their faces warm when nuzzling through the snow looking for food.
* The thinner and pointier a snowflake is, the faster it formed in the sky. Thicker, more robust flakes typically formed more slowly.
* Some icicles grow and melt repeatedly over several days, forming ridges or rings in the ice...
* ...that can be counted, like the rings inside a tree, to age the icicle!
* In 2018, a Christmas tree in Ohio was decorated with a record-breaking 6,400 candy canes.
* Refering to its circular shape, the word "wreath" comes from an Old English word for a bandage, and literally means "that which is wound around."

Solutions

RIDDLE: A north pole

ANAGRAMS

1. Advent
2. Mistletoe
3. Chimney
4. Snowman
5. Wreath
6. Calendar

December 20

What does Santa say when he's walking backwards?

Word Game

CRYPTOGRAM

In this Christmas Cryptogram, every letter in a suitably festive joke has been replaced by another. Working letter by letter, can you return the joke to its original form?

O S C A   N Q G R D   Y Q

_ H A _   _ _ _ _ Y   _ O

K C G A C ' K   R P T R K   K H R G Y ?

_ A _ _ _ ' _   _ _ _ E _   _ _ _ N D ?

W M G X P R   U M P P K !

_ I _ _ L _   B _ _ _ S !

Did you know?

MARIAH CAREY'S RECORD-BREAKING HIT

Since the early days of the Billboard charts in the 1950s, there have been a long line of festive chart-toppers and record-breakers. "White Christmas" is still one of the biggest-selling songs of all time, while even Brenda Lee's "Rockin' Around the Christmas Tree" has sold an estimated 15 million copies worldwide. (When the song reentered the charts and climbed to Number one thanks to digital downloads in 2023, it made Lee the oldest artist ever to top the Hot 100 at the age of 79, and set the record for the longest time between chart-topping singles by any artist in chart history: a total of 63 years!)

Of all the festive singles to have hit the top spot on the Billboard charts, however, few can now compare to Mariah Carey's megahit, "All I Want For Christmas Is You."

Originally released on her 1994 holiday album, *Merry Christmas*, the song proved immediately popular with fans, but was ruled ineligible for Billboard's Hot 100 chart due to it not being released as a physical single. The track received enough airplay to become a hit, however, peaking at Number six on the Adult Contemporary chart in January 1995, and returned to the charts the following Christmas. When the rules dictating chart eligibility were relaxed in 1998, however, the song embarked on an extraordinary chain of chart reappearances.

On January 8, 2000, "All I Want for Christmas Is You" made its debut on the Hot 100 six years after its release, when it climbed to a relatively lowly 83. Two years later, however, it received sufficient festive buzz to see it climb to 21, then 26 in 2013, and 35 in 2014. It finally broke the Top 20 on its return to the chart the following year, reaching number 11 in 2015, then 16 in 2016. In 2017, though, it climbed to nine, then three in 2018, and finally Number One in 2019—hitting the top spot a full 25 years after release! Incredibly, it has continued to hit the top spot on the Billboard charts every holiday season since, and its popularity shows no sign of slowing down.

Today, the song's remarkable chart history has seen it collect a slew of records. It holds the Guinness world record for the longest-running number-one song on the Billboard Global 200, is the highest-charting holiday by a solo artist, and was the first song to top the Hot 100 in six separate chart appearances. The song also set the record for the most streams on Spotify in a single 24-hour period, and on its climb to the top of the charts in 2019 gave Carey the record for most US Number Ones by a female artist in history!

Solutions

RIDDLE: "Oh! Oh! Oh!"

CRYPTOGRAM

What money do Santa's elves spend? Jingle bills!

December 21

How are Mr. and Mrs. Claus' family members known?

CHRISTMAS MAD LIB

'twas the night before a Christmas like no other...

'Twas the night before Christmas, and all through the [PLACE] *, not a creature was* [VERB-ING] *—not even a* [ANIMAL] *!*

But then someone appeared, as if by magic. It was a visitor— [FAMOUS MALE] *! He had arrived in the dead of night to drop off all the* [NOUNS] *for Christmas morning. Nobody heard or saw him, because he came in secretly, sliding down the chimney into the* [ROOM] *.*

Luckily for him, the family had left out a treat for him: a nice plate of , [FOOD] *, and , all washed down with a delicious fresh glass of* [LIQUID] *!*

After all, delivering [NOUNS] *to all houses in* [PLACE] *was thirsty work! Having finished it all, he was feeling thoroughly* [FEELING] *, and so headed off to complete his work!*

Did you know?

* The average Christmas turkey comprises a ration of white to dark meat of 7:3.
* The original title of the Christmas carol "O Holy Night" was the "Cantique de Noël."
* The first electric Christmas tree lights were used in 1882.
* Since its release in 1958, Brenda Lee's "Rockin' Around the Christmas Tree" has now been certified secen times platinum in the US.
* The tradition of putting fruit in the bottom of Christmas stockings originated in medieval France.
* The movie that would eventually become Walt Disney's *Frozen* in 2013 was originally conceived of by Walt Disney himself more than 70 years earlier in 1940!

Solutions

RIDDLE: Relative clauses!

December 22

What's the wettest, grayest animal at the North Pole?

Word Game

TWO TRUTHS AND A LIE

In each of the rounds below, two of the statements are correct, but there is one imposter. Can you guess the lie hiding among the truths?

1. THE GRINCH

A. The Grinch wasn't originally green in the book

B. The Grinch didn't originally have dog in the book

C. The Grinch wasn't originally covered in hair in the book

2. HOLLY

A. Not all holly bushes have berries

B. Not all holly berries are poisonous

C. Not all holly leaves have the same number of prickles

3. "SILENT NIGHT"

A. "Silent Night" was written in the 1800s

B. "Silent Night" is one of the world's most covered songs

C. "Silent Night" has 11 verses

Did you know?

* In the early 1900s, American photographer Wilson Bentley dedicated over 40 years of his life to painstakingly photographing individual snowflakes. Much of what we know about them today derives from his research.

* The world's most expensive Christmas tree was put up in Dubai in 2010, adorned with $11 million of Christmas decorations!

* In some parts of Wales, it is tradition to celebrate Christmas by parading a horse's skull through the town!

* Americans eat over 40 million turkeys at Thanksgiving, and a further 22 million on Christmas Day.

* Reindeer can see ultraviolet light.

* In Finland, the main Christmas meal is eaten on Christmas Eve—and traditionally features a kind of mashed, spiced, baked rutabaga dish called "lanttulaatikko."

Solutions

RIDDLE: A rain deer!

TWO TRUTHS AND A DARE

1. B. The Grinch didn't originally have a dog in the book.
   The Grinch has always had his loyal pet dog, Max. But contrary to popular belief, the original 1957 book makes no reference to the color of his fur (and in the drawings, he appears only in black and white!)
2. A. Not all holly bushes have berries
   Holly bushes are unusual in that there are male and female plants—and only the female plants produce berries.
3. C. Silent Night has 11 verses.
   In fact, it only has three.

December 23

You put me up at Christmas, admire how I look, then close the door so you can't see me. What am I?

Word Game

FINISH THE PHRASE

Do you recognize these festive phrases and sayings?
See if you can finish each line off correctly!

1. *Long lay the world in sin and error ...*

2. *Well, in Who-ville they say ... that the Grinch's small heart grew...*

3. *Snow had fallen, Snow on ...*

4. *Last Christmas I gave you my heart, but the very next day you...*

5. *Rudolph the red-nosed reindeer had a ...*

6. *May your days be merry and bright, and may all your Christmases ...*

Did you know?

* Christians didn't celebrate Christmas on December 25th right away. In fact, historians think the first December Christmastime wasn't celebrated until the 4th century CE!
* There are more than 3.5 million wild reindeer in North America.
* Old words for icicles include aquabobs, cocklebells, kinkles, and bobbytilters!
* The first Rockefeller Christmas tree was put up in 1931.
* Around one billion parcels are sent across American every Christmas.
* The "eve" in Christmas Eve has nothing to do with the Biblical Eve. It's actually just an old word for "the evening."

Solutions

RIDDLE: A Christmas wreath

FINISH THE PHRASE

1. ...pining. ("O Holy Night")
2. ...three times that day. (Dr. Seuss, *How the Grinch Stole Christmas*)
3. ...snow, snow on snow. ("In the Bleak Midwinter")
4. ...gave it away. (Wham!, "Last Christmas")
5. ...very shiny nose. ("Rudolph the Red-Nosed Reindeer")
6. ...be white. (Bing Crosby, "White Christmas")

December 24

What kind of music is everywhere on Christmas Day?

Word Game

CHRISTMAS TRIVIA QUIZ

Let's test your knowledge of all things festive with one more quick Christmas trivia quiz!

Q. ***What classic Christmas track won the Oscar for Best Original Song in 1942?***

A. "Jingle Bell Rock"
B. "White Christmas"
C. "The First Noel"
D. "Christmas Alphabet"

Q. ***What is the name of James Stewart's character in the classic Christmas movie*** **It's A Wonderful Life?**

A. George
B. Peter
C. Jack
D. Charles

Q. ***Who played Buddy the elf's biological father in the festive Will Ferrell comedy*** **Elf?**

A. Al Pacino
B. Patrick Stewart
C. Sean Connery
D. James Caan

Did you know?

THE REAL ST. NICHOLAS

His annual visit is almost here, but how much do you know about the real St. Nicholas?

The figure we know as Saint Nick was a very real person, born into a wealthy family of Greek descent in Patara, a port city in the eastern Ancient Roman province of Lycia, sometime around 270 CE. Although much about his early life is unclear, it is popularly said that Nicholas' devout Christian parents died during an outbreak of an unknown disease when he was still relatively young, leaving their fortune to him. Following what he understood of the teachings of Jesus, Nicholas dedicated his life to God and joined the church, all the while using his great fortune to making the lives of the sick and needy in Lycia better.

While still a young man, Nicholas was made bishop of Myra, another city on the coast of Lycia, where tales of his boundless generosity and concern for the children and the sick became known far and wide. Many of the tales of Nicholas' time in Myra have since gone down in history as miracles: when word reached him that three children had been killed, for instance, Nicholas reportedly prayed for their souls and the trio came back to life. (Because their bodies had been held in barrels, Nicholas is often portrayed standing in a wooden tub in images and stained glass windows, and is even venerated today as the patron saint of coopers!)

Over time, however, the world in which Nicholas found himself began to sour, and the new Roman Emperor Diocletian embarked on a ruthless persecution of Christians across the Roman empire in the early 300s CE. Refusing to renounce his faith, Nicholas was exiled, and eventually imprisoned. He remained there until his release under Constantine the Great, and went on to take part in the monumental Council of Nicaea—a council of early Christian bishops and clergymen—in the Roman city of Nicaea (in modern-day Turkey) in 325.

Having returned to Myra as bishop, Nicholas died there in 343 CE, and was buried in his cathedral church. His grave soon became associated with further miracles, and as a cult of devotion emerged around him and the anniversary of his death—December 6, not December 25 as some stories claim!—became a major feast day in many Christian countries, including the Netherlands.

In fact, it is his old Dutch name, *Sinter Niklaas*—along with his lifelong benevolence, and fondness for bestowing gifts on his parishioners—that eventually gave us our tales of Santa Claus!

Solutions

RIDDLE: Rapping!

CHRISTMAS TRIVIA QUIZ

1. B. "White Christmas."
   Written for the movie *Holiday Inn*, the song won songwriter Irving Berlin his first and only Oscar. Oddly, the song would go on to inspire the movie *White Christmas* in 1954, for which Berlin wrote the song "Count your Blessings," and went on to be nominated for another Oscar!
2. A. George.
   Stewart's character is named George Bailey.
3. D. James Caan.
   The movie was originally written in the mid 1990s with plans for Jim Carrey to take on the title role, before Will Ferrell took over the project in 2003.

Conclusion

Merry Christmas!

Your Christmas countdown is now at an end, and the big day itself is finally here. Hopefully this holiday season has brought you much joy, light, and celebration—and hopefully, this collection of trivia, riddles, facts, and games has brought you a daily dose of fun too!

But if you've reached the end of this Advent Calendar, then that must mean it's Christmas morning! (Or perhaps, that Christmas morning is just a few hotly anticipated hours away, right?!) So, either it's time to celebrate, or it's time for some last-minute preparations... Either way, it's about time you put this book down and get on with your day!

Have a very happy Christmas!

Printed in Dunstable, United Kingdom

73630608R00057